Mark Hornstein

Playing Chess with Bess

A first Introduction to the Game of Kings for young children

Illustrations by Tali Doron

English: Elana Gotkine and Mark Granat

Editing: GX Localizations Ltd.
Graphics: Studio Taliron

Introduction

As parents, we are not always aware of our children's ability to grasp and learn new things, including things that seem complicated or difficult.

I allowed myself to write a book about learning to play chess, specifically for young children, with the full belief in their wondrous ability to learn new things, and in the parents' ability to be great teachers.

The game of chess is an excellent tool for developing cognitive abilities and social skills.

This book is designed for a gradual introduction to the game of chess: getting to know the board and pieces, acquiring the basic knowledge about the pieces and their moves, all through pictures and rhyme.

I hope you will enjoy this book with your child. The aim is not to transform them into Chess masters, but to give them a taste, and awaken in them a desire to play and learn more about this special game.

The instructions are given in masculine form but refer to both genders.

Guide for Parents

It is recommended that you read through this book and the guidelines for parents before reading it to your child.

I recommend reading the book with a chess board and pieces available (ideally a big board and pieces, so your child won't put them in his mouth). Each time you introduce a new piece, you can give it to the child to hold, introduce your child to the piece, and place it down on the board. Ideally, this should be done when your child is relaxed and not too tired, away from distractions such as television, music etc.

For those of you who are not familiar with the rules of the game, you can find explanations and more information by the US Chess Federation:
http://main.uschess.org/

One day, Bess's dad, when he arrived home,
Had a box in his arms. From where did it come?
He stopped and he smiled. "What's that, Dad"? asked Bess.
"This," said her dad "is a game we call Chess."
"Chess? Chess? Is that what you said?"
Replied pretty Bess with a shake of her head.
Her dad smiled and said, "Come, sit with me Bess.
I'm going to explain to you how to play Chess."

Dad opened the box, and what a surprise!
Pieces galore – each its own shape and size
Black and white pieces, so many of them
Some shaped like animals, and others like men
"What are all these pieces? Are they little dolls?"
"No, Bess, they are pieces with all different roles.
Hold on and I'll answer each question you ask.
Each of the pieces has its own special task"

Guidelines for parents:
At this point I suggest you open the box and take out the pieces, but don't give
them to your child yet, keep them hidden for later.

Dad took out the pieces, turned the board and revealed
Black and white squares "It's a battle field"
Dad explained, "In Chess we play like we fight
In a game of war of black against white"

Dad asked, "Do you see how many squares that there are?
Let us count, exactly, how wide and how far."
They counted together from each side to side,
"Eight this way! Eight there!",
Bess smartly replied

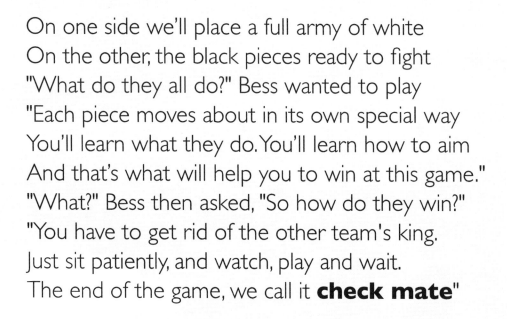

On one side we'll place a full army of white
On the other, the black pieces ready to fight
"What do they all do?" Bess wanted to play
"Each piece moves about in its own special way
You'll learn what they do. You'll learn how to aim
And that's what will help you to win at this game."
"What?" Bess then asked, "So how do they win?"
"You have to get rid of the other team's king.
Just sit patiently, and watch, play and wait.
The end of the game, we call it **check mate**"

Guidelines for parents:
Take out the pieces and put them on the board so they are arranged in two camps
at either ends of the board. There is no need to set the board up correctly, but
rather to show your child that there are two teams facing one another - black
against white

Dad showed Bess the pawns that belong to each team
These are the foot soldiers, eager and keen.

"We are eight brave pawns, though we appear small
We fend for the King so that he will not fall
One square right in front, that is all we can step
But if we get to the end, we can alter our shape."

Guidelines to parents:
Take out the pawns (not the other pieces), and introduce your child to them. Allow him
to hold the pawn and put it down on the board. Afterwards, show him how it moves.

Next Dad took two bishops, one black and one white
"Let's see what these two have to do in this fight"

"We are two eager bishops, we run and we pray,
Moving diagonally, that's just how we play
One moves on the black, the other on white
We can move any distance! Yes, you'll get it right."

Guidelines for parents:
At this point, you can introduce your child to the bishops (only take these pieces out).
Choose one white and one black - encourage your child to "befriend" them, and put them
down on the board. Show him how they move diagonally, with one on white and the
other on black.

"And these two," said Dad, "are quite special forces.
We call them the knights, but they look just like horses!"

"Neigh! Neigh! good Sir Knight, just where are you rushing?
Knights jump! We leap right over pieces – no pushing
Two squares to the front, then one to the side
This neat airborne move, it just has to be tried"

Guidelines for parents:
At this point introduce your child to the knights. Choose one white and one black. Let your child have a look at them, and then encourage him to put them on the board. Show him their special move. You can put another piece on the board to show your child how the knight jumps over other pieces.

"And now what is this?"
Bess wanted to know
"It looks like a castle,
but it's really quite low."
"Oh right," said Dad,
"I will give you a clue.
This rook's for defense,
and each team has just two."

"We are the two rooks, we stand at each end
We patiently watch, and wait to defend
In a straight line we move in any direction
And we offer the king our special protection
We can move any distance, to attack or defend
And often you'll see us still here at the end!"

Guidelines for parents:
Now introduce your child to the rooks, one white and one black. The child can
play with them and then put them onto the board. The parents should place a rook
in each corner and show the child how it moves in vertically and horizontally.

And now we must meet with Her Highness the Queen

The most powerful piece you will ever have seen,
Take one look at her, she is strong in attack
She can move left and right, to the front and the back
And diagonally too – it's close to perfection
She can go any distance, in every direction!

Guidelines for parents
At this point, take out the black and white queens and show them to your child. They should put the queens on the board, and show them how they move. You should emphasize that they can move in every direction.

"And the last of them all", said Dad, "is the King."
There wouldn't be much of a game without him.
He stands at the rear, on his head a great crown,
He watches the game-play unfold with a frown

The King is the one on whom all does depend
And for whom every piece gives its life to defend
I am certain that you, Bess would like to know why
"Tell me the big deal about that guy" you cry
Because if the King falls, the game will be done
The player that sits over there will have won
So we have to protect him no matter the cost
For if we do not then the game will be lost.

Guidelines for parents
It's time to show your child the black and white kings. Let him put them on the board,
and show him how they move. Emphasize the importance of the king, and the need
to protect him.

So now my dear Bess,
You have met them all
The King,
and Her Highness the Queen,
Standing tall
Two Rooks and two Bishops,
Eight Pawns and two Knights
All eager to play, and ready to fight!
Now that you know how to play and to win
Would you like to play? Are you set to begin?

Made in the USA
Charleston, SC
13 January 2012